1

MAKE EXHIBITIONS WORK

Set up a sell-out!

Graeme Smith

PUBLISHED ON AMAZON.com
by
LABYRINTH BOOKS

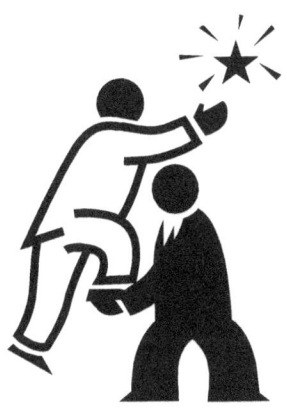

DEDICATION:

This book is dedicated to my family.
Hele-ly (Ly).
      my wife:

Ingrid.
      our daughter:

Marie.
      my former wife:

Fiona, Natalie and Michael
      our children:

Georgie
      Michael's wife:

Pearl, Kiki and Martha.
      their children:

They have had to put up with me for many years and I thank them for that.
I hope this book gives them an insight into what has occupied me much of the time.
They have all achieved worthwhile and interesting careers in the absence of much help from me.
I congratulate them for their achievements.

THANKS:

I greatly appreciate the contribution made to this book by comments and suggestions from:

Mike Barr – Adelaide, Australia

Richard Bruland - Los Angeles, USA

Tracey Creighton - Merimbula, Australia

Evelyn Dunphy – Maine, USA

Geoff Fellows – Wagga Wagga, Australia

Michelle Grace - Brisbane, Australia

Leanne Halls – North Sydney, Australia

Heidi Jeffries – Ferny Hills, Australia

Kathy Kay Voysey - Mudgee, Australia.

Vincent Miller - 'Australian Artist' and 'International Artist.

John Newell - Ontario, Canada

David Voigt – Yarramalong, Australia.

HOW TO USE THIS BOOK.

First think - then do.
Usually people don't think through things to the level they need to.
Because of that, they have projects instead of tasks on their "to do" list.
That leads to procrastination as it hasn't been broken down to a task level.

So go through your book once to understand it.
Go through it again.

Then start at the idea you would like to implement first.
Make notes of the steps you will need to take and the resources required.
Use the notes to create a step by step system for implementing the guide.
Often you won't refer back to an original, as you've created YOUR system.

The first question you ask and answer is "Why is this being done?"
How does this align with where you want to get to?
What are the strategic implications of doing this?
Does this fit with getting to a goal in the shortest and fastest time?

What would it be like if it were totally successful?
Define it - what is success for this project and how will you know?

Now brainstorm all the tasks that are involved in your project.
It's important not to go linear too fast with this.
By linear, I mean step one, step two, step three, and step four.
You end up cutting off options.
Plan step one, two, and three, a specific step that might be number four.
If you start steps quickly, other ways of one, two or three may not appear.

The first third of any brainstorming session is really easy.
Just come up with lots of ideas.
The second third is challenging - go through ideas - see where they lead.
Then push yourself to think a little bit outside the box.
That's often where the big idea is!

That's where the most powerful way to get a project done fastest - is.
Most people never get to that level and short-change themselves.
Then their project takes longer and they also procrastinate.
This final brainstorming part of the equation is incredibly important.

Once you fully brainstorm put your options into a linear sequence.
Then you can figure out what you've overlooked.
Everything becomes obvious as you get your tasks in order.
Now add missing steps and you have laid out your task list for this project.

Once you've organized the tasks into a linear process decide:
What things can you start immediately?
What can be started that is not dependent on things to occur before them?
Obviously that is step one.
Step five or six or twenty don't really rely on anything else to get done.
You can get started on them right away too.

Now use a folder.
Write things you think of at the time and cross off things as you do them.
Add in stuff that is relevant from time to time.

WHAT IS MARKETING?

Marketing is the process of finding buyers AND making sales
It is exactly the same process no matter what is being sold!
In some cases the process is simple like selling apples at a roadside stall.
It can be complex like selling aero-planes for a government's air-force.
Most, including selling artworks, is somewhere in between these poles.

Think about fishing and you'll understand marketing.
Does a fisherman catch anything out in a desert?
NO, for there are simply no fish there.

You must market where there are possible buyers.
A fisherman must go where the fish are – where there is water.
That's a start but there are still no fish in a swimming pool are there?
They need to be in the right kind of water – a river, lake or at sea.

But different fish swim in different waters!
Sharks and marlin are in the ocean, while bream live mainly in rivers.
Likewise you must know who you are targeting with your marketing.
Will it be businesses, first home buyers, investors or what?
Each will need a different marketing program.

OK you are now in the right water for the kind of fish you are after!
Some species are nocturnal and they will not be caught during the day.
Your marketing needs to be when the target is likely to be most receptive.
Will it be at work, nights or weekends?

You are at the right place and time so how do you catch the fish?
Usually you'll have a fishing rod.
Is it the right kind for the fish you want to catch?
You won't catch a shark with the kind of rod that takes a trout!
Your marketing must be attractive to the people you are after.

Do you have the right bait?
Again different bait attracts different fish.
A carcass for the shark but just a worm for many other species.
Can you provide something that your target market will find attractive?

But throwing any bait into the water catches nothing at all!
The bait must be attached to a hook.
Without the fish taking the hook there is no catch.
Different hooks are needed for different kinds of fish.

Different hooks are also needed for different markets.
The right hook gets your market to take the next step to a purchase.
But this only needs to be a little step.
But hooks only catch the fish.

They're in water, not your boat or beach, a hook is the end of a line.
What is your line like, is it strong enough you the fish you are after?
Again this varies for the kind of fish.

How do you get your prospect to seriously consider what you sell?
For someone buying a print it will not need to be sophisticated.
But selling an original Renoir will be considerably more complicated.

That still no fish for the line has to have a reel for that to happen.
Again different reels for different fish.
The right reel allows you to bring the fish to the end of your fishing line.
But it's still not in the boat is it?

You must lift the fish out of the water into your boat or onto a beach.
Fishing nets do this so now you have your catch.
The fish is yours to do what you want with.

You can even sell the fish but who might want to buy?
It could be someone who sells fish for food or live for a fish-tank or pool.
They could even be for re-stocking natural water places.

Where can you find them?

You must look where the fish buyers are!

Follow the path of the fisherman.

And eventually you have a prospect asking can they buy.

You have made a sale AND you can make more sales the same way.

Making the sale is a five step process.

In order you work from the top through to the bottom group.

> **SUSPECTS** are people who possibly want what you have for sale.
>
> **PROSPECTS** are people likely to want what you have for sale.
>
> **BUYERS** are those who have bought what you are selling.
>
> **REPEAT BUYERS** continue to buy what you sell.
>
> **ADVOCATES** help you sell to others.

The reverse sequence is the order of importance to your sales.

INDEX: MAKE EXHIBITIONS WORK

Chapter One: Your career vision.

1. Do you have a career vision?
2. It can be done.
3. But there is no short cut.
4. Exhibitions represent an opportunity for multiple sales.
5. Plan for exhibition success.
6. Exhibitions cost money.

1. Do you have a career vision?

Most artists tend to focus on an individual painting.
An exhibition is a collection of those paintings.

But what if the focus was on the exhibition.
And it was just one of a series of exhibitions?
Then there would be a different mind-set wouldn't there?
How you approach exhibitions is an extension of this thinking.
Do you do that?

Then a career can be an ongoing stream of exhibitions.
Be pro-active about generating this income stream if you know what to do.
A successful artist should have this knowledge.
Can you identify the characteristics necessary for a sell-out exhibition?
Most artists dont even believe this is possible so they don't think about it!

But it shouldn't matter what you paint for artwork doesn't sell itself.
If it did, you'd be able to hang work anywhere and people would buy it.
There needs to be a correlation between what you do and how it is sold.
But obviously something is done to make sell-out exhibitions happen.

But one artist having a sell-out exhibition doesn't prove anything.
That depends on special knowledge, contacts, opportunities they have.
It's people like you who have to have the sell-out exhibitions.
If you are somewhat skeptical that's understandable.

The key element is people willing to buy your work.
Then these people can be leveraged into major career momentum.
You need sales and marketing strategies major galleries give main artists.
Not all galleries do this.
MANY do **NOT KNOW** what to do and you must assume this is likely.

Sales in a well-known gallery are quite public.
That's a launch pad for continued success and sustained artistic career.
So you need a marketing campaign aimed at the gallery of your choice.

This is not necessarily what most other artists say you should do.
BUT someone has to do it.
Otherwise you will be exhibiting at a gallery that doesn't know what to do.

There's a lot of day to day stuff in any profession, including artist.
Meeting people, phone calls, enter competitions, framing, finances, etc.
The more successful you are the more of it there is.
You do all this yourself initially but eventually you need an agent.
But by then you'll know exactly what you want them to do.
So instead of the agent telling you what they want.
You'll find one who does what you want.

2. It can be done.

I opened a gallery and after a few years exhibited my own work.
In one of those early exhibitions I had 50 works and sold the lot!
But it took many years before I worked out why that happened.
I tried all sorts of strategies to replicate that result.
Not just with my own works but other artists too.

Here is the lead-up to one of my later exhibition experiences.
In 1988 I went to the Wagga Gold Cup race meeting where I live.
THE major horse race of the year here and also an important social event.
I hadn't previously been even though I'd lived here for 11 years (then).
I wasn't particularly interested in horse racing (gallops).
One of our major artists was visiting in a lead up to his exhibition.
So we went to the Gold Cup.

Well I was fascinated by the spectacle.
There were the jockeys, all in their brilliant colours.
What I hadn't realised before was how muscular they all were.
I guess you do have to be strong to keep control of those powerful horses.
Another thing I didn't realise was the way they swaggered.
Elsewhere they might be little people but at the track they were the kings.

The bookies immaculately dressed like a flashback to a past era.
They were still wearing suits from the 50's - amazing!
And the punters were dressed in the latest fashion with matching accessories
Or at the other end of fashions with thongs, shorts and T shirts.

I thought about this and understood the fascination of the race track.
Artists for centuries have been enthralled by the colour, variety and action.
Degas is of course well known but there have been many others.
I also realised that it had been a long time since I last painted a person.
In recent years I had focused on landscapes and abstract paintings.
I liked painting people but it had been a long time since I had done any.
I thought I might have a go at people at the races for a series of paintings.

A few weeks later I met the racing administrators to discuss the idea.
They were enthusiastic and offered co-operation to help me.
I was given access to places few punters ever get to visit.
The jockey's room before a race, and the weigh in room after a race.
A close view of the horses in the starting stalls was also permitted.
I could go wherever I like during a meeting if I kept out of the way.

I thought what to do with the paintings once they were completed.
There would be enough works for an exhibition, so that was a project.
I already had a venue, my gallery, so that was no problem.
But I needed the likely buyers (don't we all).
So I invited the chairman of the racing club to open the exhibition.
His committee was also invited and my racing exhibition was set to go.

I painted the works and they turned out fine (as I expected).
Some were modestly sized and others smaller.
A number of the smaller ones were watercolours.
A medium I hadn't used for 20 years, to a small extent in my art course.
I was quite pleased with how they turned out.
I could've become a water colour artist, but I haven't done any since.

The exhibition was just like everyone else's - I didn't sell anything!
This surprised me, just as other artists who produced their best works.
My exhibition was in my gallery **AND** past exhibitions successful.
As usual people liked the paintings but this time just didn't buy.

What had I done wrong?
The works were OK so the marketing was where I looked for solutions.
I now had a framed exhibition of works still to sell.

The obvious buyers were the people who go to the races.
So once more I met with the racing administration.
An exhibition of racing paintings at the racecourse on Melbourne Cup day.
It's the biggest race event in Australia with a local meeting held as well.
This meeting was their second biggest after the Wagga Gold Cup.

I should be able to do better for the right people would see the works.
Well what happened this time?
I had lots of interest and viewers could identify the people in the paintings.
Again they liked what they saw.
This was a relief as when I started I realized I had to paint horses.
I hadn't thought about that for my focus was on the people at the races.

How did the sales go then?
I sold one small watercolour to a bookmaker, the subject of the painting.
A bit further down the track I sold one of the major paintings.
It was of the grandstand with a crowd of people viewing the races.
It was in a TV ad on the next Melbourne Cup Day.
I used it to attract the attention of the likely viewers in that time slot.
One viewer saw the painting, rang up and bought it - just like that!

I abstracted some, painted over others, sold some and have the rest.
But I learned something which eventually came together years later.

A common mistake is thinking people only had to see works to buy.
Have you done that?
Someone has to sell those works and that's what I should have done.

3. But there is no short cut.

Artists think a gallery exhibition as the start of a professional career!
Sooner or later they approach a gallery to sell and/or exhibit their work.
Usually they'd like an exhibition, and need a gallery to do this?
That's the most common reason but least likely for a satisfactory outcome.

Galleries exist to make money for its owner and artists who exhibit.
Holding exhibitions is one way this is done.
Done right they are an opportunity for bulk sales.
Galleries are NOT there to provide artists with exhibition spaces.
Particularly if they feel like having an exhibition just to show their work!
When I had a gallery it was no different.

Gallery visitors have long memories.
Their first impressions of your work will be the ones that are strongest.
But what do they actually remember?
Following an exhibition they remember how many were sold and little else!

The memories stay, no matter what you do, even years later.
It's tough, but that's how it is.

Artists think a gallery exhibition begins a professional career!
It is **BUT** only if it is successful!
Otherwise your career will continue as it began as an unsuccessful artist.

A professional artist doesn't just produce paintings.
You sell, market, and do all tasks other small business people perform.
The more successful you are the more of this there is to do!
You could be frightened at the money you're going to have to earn.
Each and every year you are in business.

It's easy to lose direction though.
Before my gallery days I went to an exhibition at a major Sydney gallery.
The artist was an excellent impressionist artist whose work was popular.

But he was also a very creative person.
His exhibition comprised abstract works in black and white.
They were accompanied by his poetry.
He didn't sell any which set his professional career back years!

I never forgot that lesson particularly years later in my own gallery.
I didn't want any surprises for my clients from my artists.
That is one of the main ways an artist loses career momentum!
They get bored with their present activity and change direction.

4. Why are exhibitions so important?

Exhibitions are a chnce for multiple sales, now and in the future.
There is really no readily available alternative.
Publicity and gallery space focus is on an artist, a group, or type of work.
For sufficient time to enhance the sales outcome.

The objective is to sell as many works as possible.
Exhibition marketing takes advantage of known buyer behaviour patterns.
If successful, results can exceed other sales by a huge margin.
It's definitely worth being involved in, but it must be done properly to work.

Bulk sales make earning a living by being an artist possible.
Selling the occasional painting now and then can earn money.
Unless the works are highly priced, you need another source of income.

Hobby artists show, but professionals sell.
Exhibitions are not merely a way of showing people your work.
Exhibitions are staged to sell as many works as possible at one time.
That means the aim of **ANY** exhibition is to **SELL the LOT**.

So how important is selling to you?
Do you leave the selling to a gallery, or art show volunteers?
If our works don't sell, we're out of the art business - isn't that important?
A consequence of the so-called selling barriers is people give up too soon.
Harvard University research shows salespeople give up after two attempts.
The research said most purchases are after five (or more) non-closures.
Those figures are averages so there are wide variations in the statistics.

Less significant lower priced items may be bought at first encounter.
BUT this is buying at a supermarket.

The more complex and expensive to a buyer.
The more sales encounters are needed.
Complex sales are not just about money but also status.

5. Plan for your exhibition success.

Do most people actually buy an artwork the first time they see it?
In my gallery people often visited a number of times before a decision.
Timing, persistence and patience are the keys to successful selling.

Notice there are few sales at an exhibition after the opening?
I certainly have for whilst the occasional exhibition sells then, most do not.
Those that do are low cost exhibitions, or by previously unknown artists.
Even then not many works are sold, just more than beforehand.
The person most likely to buy then is often artistically unsophisticated.

At my gallery for some years I kept records of when sales took place.
Most happened before the Opening (not even at the Opening).
We found, as other galleries, selling before an opening increased sales.
This is particularly true when the artist is well known and popular.
A reason was each buyer believes they're getting in before anyone else.
Psychologically it's the best time for selling artworks.

There are really two phases to an exhibition.
The selling phase and the rest of the exhibition.

Selling commences when you agree to exhibit.
It gathers momentum in the month or two before the exhibition.
When the works are delivered actual selling can commence.
This continues to accelerate when the works are hung.

The Sales Phase is more usually called the Preview Period.
During this time early buying is encouraged.
Use special preview price, 'hot seats', early notification to keen buyers.

Emails reinforce the focus.
This ends when the exhibition opens to the public.
The activity is focused on individuals who might buy.

The main focus of marketing exhibitions is to generate multiple sales.
Incentive pricing is designed to reward early buyers.
The best (lowest) price is given to the preview period buyers.
Those who buy later in an exhibition pay most.

Pricing is thus used as a tactic to encourage earlier decision making.
It encourages people to buy when you want them to rather than take time.

The initial price (lowest) must be considered carefully.
This is the ordinary selling price, but sometimes it could be less.

A later exhibition price is higher.
Just how much depends on you and the gallery.
It may be a token amount or vary according to the price of the works.
At my gallery we had a 10% difference between the prices.

The exhibition opening reception completes the selling phase.
Most works are sold by this time, particularly for popular artists.
This doesn't mean no effort later, but not the same intensity or focus.

The Future Sales Phase is more often called the Exhibition Period.
Exhibition Opening or Reception transitions from sales to public display.
The exhibition phase is when future sales prospects can be identified.
General publicity during the exhibition is more likely to attract such people.
How work is displayed reflects differences between the phases (price too).

Different things are done in the selling phase and future sales period.
Regular clients are targeted in the selling phase.
In the future sales phase general advertising is used for new prospects.

From the Opening to the end of an exhibition is to capture prospects.
They're for your **NEXT** exhibition.
People come in to see what the work is like, without expecting to buy.
It is an important period, although this does not show up in $ at the time.
This is the future sales phase.

You are educating people about prices for your NEXT exhibition.
That's when they will be higher (won't they?).
The educational is better started with works that didn't sell this time.
Than with a whole bunch of new works in the next exhibition.
Incentive to buy early and set price expectation ahead of future exhibitions.

I later wrote a guide for artists to have their own sell-out exhibition.
There was feedback of successful exhibition outcomes.
This career guide is an update of that earlier one.

6. Here's an email I received from Richard Rogers in 2009

Thought Id let you know how I went.
With the 'Off the Beaten Track' exhibition!

I read one of your articles about planning a sellout exhibition.
That was a completely new thought to me - what a powerful idea!
Most artists plan exhibitions and hope they sell.
Very few would actually plan to have a sellout.

I took your advice and that's what I began to plan and work for.
I produced 20 paintings, domestic size, beautifully frame.
And priced for anyone to afford.
I had a beautiful catalogue printed.

I also did a lot of work making connections.
I built my database and promoting the exhibition.

Nicky Downer, wife of former Foreign Minister, opened exhibition.
Around one hundred and twenty people attended.

10 of the paintings sold before the official opening.
That was a result of the catalogue mail-out.

5 more were sold at the opening and 3 more while the exhibition ran.
An unsold work I left at the Hahndorf Academy.
This was where the exhibition was held.
It sold a few days later. (I'm still going to count that in the sales.)

That makes 19 out of 20 paintings that sold ... a 95% sell-out.
I paid my sister for some of the work she did for me.
I'll be donating 10% of exhibition proceeds to the Flying Doctor Service. Add other expenses catering, postage, framing, printing, gallery fees.
I'll come very close to breaking even.

OK, it wasn't been a complete sell-out.
But 95% is still pretty impressive.
And I have gained a lot through the exercise.
My credibility and standing as a professional artist is greatly enhanced;

I've learnt so much that I can use again in the future;
My data base is bigger and better;
The catalogue will be an advert for me and my work for years to come.
It has already opened a couple of doors for me.
This has been an important step in my career.

Thank you Graeme for your inspiration.
The idea that I could have a sell-out exhibition.
Thank you for all your suggestions about how I could make that happen.
It worked.

Please feel free to use any part of this email as an endorsement.

Chapter Two: Planning ahead.

1. **Where will you exhibit for the best result?**
2. **What will your sell-out exhibition contain?**
3. **Pricing for your sell-out exhibition.**

1. Where will you exhibit for the best result?

Where would you like your sell-out exhibition to take place?
Start from the top, pick the very best, most suitable gallery you can think of.
There should be a certain amount of prestige involved.
It should be in a city not too far from you and sell works roughly like yours.
Once you've decided on your gallery, you can start getting used to the idea.

There're 2 galleries, those who will take your work and those who won't.
You don't need the first as they're desperate and unsuccessful.
They'll go out of business probably suddenly.
The owner is probably honest and well-intentioned but has no money.
They can't promote without money and really don't know what to do anyway.

The other gallery owners don't need you – yet!
They're in business so with the right approach you can enter their artist ranks.
You only need to represent a business opportunity for them.
They've been around for some time.
Their sales techniques are well honed and work.

Their loyalty is to artists they already represent.
They're **NOT** looking for new artists but clients interested in their focus.

Don't approach them as an artist yet.
A little further down the track you'll need to sell the exhibition to the gallery.
But not yet.
If your groundwork has been properly laid, you'll go well.

Visit your chosen gallery as a potential buyer.

Do not worry about whether they will want to exhibit your work or not.

Ask about someone who interested in buying wok like yours might ask.

What if your chosen gallery is too far away?

Well you might still start there.

But it's more likely to be where you'll go for exhibition number two.

That will be for making money (as well as a sell-out).

2. What works will you have in your sell-out exhibition?

A professional artist can work to any scale.
An assumption is quality lies in the content of the work rather than its scale.
Size variations let you consider art business without compromising integrity.
Most artists paint and **THEN** consider the price.
Most professional artists relate their prices to different sizes.

BEFORE you START consider size of works and how it relates to price.
Then decide the size of your paper, plate, board or canvas.
This is an important concept, the understanding of which is essential.

Another important consideration is the number of sizes you work in.
The sizes available can be limited and then varied as a marketing strategy.
There's a direct relationship between the size of a work and the cost too.
Stretchers, canvas, paper, paint, costs change according to size or amount.
A small work doesn't cost too much to frame.
But the frame proportion of the total price is usually high.

But there's still value in small works, even if the frame reduces profit.
Small paintings can be used to open up a market for your work.
Once that has been done then the sizes (and prices) can be increased.
Then you start to reap a better reward for your efforts.
This is the basis of the sell-out exhibition strategy.

Controlled sizes you can make more effective framing cost choices too.
Standard frame and painting sizes mean you can re-use frames.
Standardize frame style as you discover which frames look and sell the best.
Then you've works in a number of places, presented well and optimum sizes.
They have not cost you any more than necessary for framing.

Then size can be used as a marketing tool.
Particularly if you establish a clear price/size relationship in people's minds.
It's logical because **ALL** works put on sale should be up to your standard.

Then it is possible to use various combinations as a marketing device.
With the variations you adjust price over time without people being aware.
You can leave out size 'B' from an exhibition one year at a particular venue.
Next exhibition at the venue size B works re-appear but a higher price-tag.
Mix combinations over years and steadily work your way up the price scale.
You'll need to modify the number of works of a size that are for sale too.

3. Pricing for your sell-out exhibition.

Exhibitions are usually regular and scheduled.
So you must save new works for any exhibition.
Bulk sales make earning a living as an artist possible.
There is really no readily available alternative.

Exhibitions are carefully staged promotions.
They are designed to sell as many of your works as possible at the one time.
That means the aim of **ANY** exhibition is to **SELL the LOT**.

Use your old prices for works you currently have.
This will help your chances of a sell-out with your **NEW** works.
That's why those prices should be **LESS** than your present pricing structure.

The lower exhibition prices will make your exhibition more attractive.
Particularly to those who bought at your present price, or who know about it.
Your current prices are part of the 'old' artist so you'll be leaving that behind.
They have nothing to do with the artist who'll become rich and famous.

Would you be prepared to burn all the old works you have right now?
If you're moving forward you would be as the past is lead in the saddle-bags!

Now let's apply these ideas to your forthcoming sell-out exhibitions.
Gallery 1 is your first venue, Gallery 2 is the next one and Gallery 3 the third.
None of these galleries have previously been exhibited at.

See next page:

YEAR	GALLERY 1	GALLERY 2	GALLERY 3
One	5xB@$600		
	5xC@$750		
	5xD@$1000		
Two	10xA@$600	10XA@$525	
	5xC@$800	5xB@$750	
Three	5XA@$750	10XA@$675	10XA@$600
	5XB@$800	5XC@$900	5XB@$800
	5XC@$975		
Four	10XB@$1125	5XA@$825	10XA@$750
	5XC@$1500	5XB@$825	5XC@$975
	5XD@$1725	5XC@$1359	5XD@$1200
		5XD@41500	

A, B, C, D, and E are different sized original works.

The prices shown are just numbers.
They do not represent recommendations about what you should charge.
They only illustrate how they might relate to one another.

This principle works for any artworks.
BUT the numbers might be different for oils compared to drawings.
They could vary between portraits and landscapes as well - you decide.
The price moved up at all venues and later venues compared to earlier ones.

Consider modified pricing at $100, $200, $500 and $1000 thresholds.
It's recommended you hold prices under these levels longer than anticipated.
Then skip to a higher price than logical if even steps were maintained.
Here's where you make up for holding the price down earlier.

Price every exhibition according to these principles.
If the first at each venue is a success (all sell).
It's possible to have a continuing income stream from successful exhibitions.

Now, just get started with those great paintings.

But don't take any of them anywhere until they're all finished.

Even then it will only be to the photographer (who could come to you).

Chapter Three: Start the sell-out!

1. Here's an overview of how that is done.

There are three phases to achieving a sell-out exhibition.
Paint the works (about 20) with careful consideration to the size of the works.
Sell the exhibition to the gallery (can't start until most of the works are ready).
Sell the exhibition for the gallery (they won't for unknown artists so you must).

You know how long the first phase will take.
The other two phases could easily take three months.
They will involve quite a deal of non-painting time by you.

At the end of a first sell-out exhibition at a prestige gallery you have:
No works
No money
No debt

Then you get started on sell-out exhibition no 2.
Again there are three phases:
Painting the works (about 20 or perhaps a few more).
Selling the exhibition to the gallery but only if it's a new gallery.
This will be easier because of the first sell-out exhibition.
The gallery will be keen to cash in on your slightly higher prices.

At the end of a second sell out exhibition at the same gallery you have:
No works
Some money (a few more works, slightly higher prices and reduced costs)
No debt

Now you get started on sell-out exhibition no 3.
Again there are three phases:
Painting the works (about 20 or perhaps more, with some a little larger).
This will be even easier because of your track record.
It might be at one of the first two galleries, who'll already have keen buyers.
Selling the exhibition by the gallery.

At the end of a third sell out exhibition at a prestige gallery you have:
No works
Even more money (slightly higher prices again).
Plus some larger works at even higher prices, with minimal costs.
No debt

This process repeats, limited by the number of works produced.
So all you have to do is paint and the prices will keep moving up.
They reach a stage where you are embarrassed by the dollars they bring in.

2. Now start painting

Paint with SINCERITY and INTEGRITY!
In other words paint because there's something you want to paint.
Or an idea you want to develop, or something you want to try.
Or for anything intrinsic to the work and your experience.

Any other reason and it is hard to maintain motivation and enthusiasm.
Particularly in the long term (as a career should be).

Paint around 20 or so works (not too large, not too small)?
They'll be the best you've ever done,
That's because your whole artistic future is linked to these works.

It is not possible to have a sell-out exhibition without works to sell.
They need to be put aside and you might do other work just to earn money.
If so that must not eat into your time too much.
An alternative income source is very helpful.

Cut major works (large) right out, even for the sell-out exhibition.
They just take too much time.
They're also harder to sell (now).
Eventually you'll do those again and sell them as well.
That will be when you are capitalizing on your career momentum.

Those exhibition paintings are the best you've ever done.
There are no really large works.
Largest paintings not too big, small ones half that and one or two between.

The sizes are you easily sell at an average price of about $500 each.
You earn a gross of $10,000 when you sell 20 works.
This could be less than your current prices.
But you need that to cover your costs though.

Don't forget this exhibition is about selling the lot.
Making money comes **AFTER** that beginning.

Your professional future (money & fame) depends on these paintings.
So the works should not just be your best, they should be uniquely yours.
Each one should have your particular style embedded in it.
All works are obviously by the same artist without looking at the signature!
Think of a van Gough exhibition and you'll have the idea.

20 works are because much less is hardly an exhibition.
A couple less may be OK, but not too many.
On the other hand there's no need for more.
Every extra work is another you need to sell.
From that point of view the fewer works the better.

About 20, is a balance between being enough to comprise an exhibition.
And not too many to actually sell.
In addition it's a good number for promotional purposes.

Before any works are sold, you spend money on promotional material.
This will not be cheap.
Costs will be around $5000, mainly framing, printing and photography.
The balance of the income from the exhibition will be the gallery's share.

I cannot be exact about these amounts.
So if you want to budget for more that is sensible.
You will recover all this from exhibition sales.

There's no need to frame the works initially.
But eventually you'll have to do this.
Arrange with your framer to delay payment until after the exhibition.

A professional artist is a self-employed business person.
So whatever you do, will cost money which is in advance of it being earned.
A successful business person, even artist, is impossible without spending.

3. So where are the buyers?

Go to the big city where the gallery is you intend to exhibit and sell at.
Buy and read the newspapers from this city, which might even be your own.
In particular look through the local news and social pages.

Make a list of people who seem to be the most important people there.
They probably own businesses, or are CEO's of major companies.
Perhaps they do good things, or attend interesting events, etc.

Do this for a month and you have most key people from the newspaper.
Check your list against the actual news pages.
Delete anyone who is in trouble.
The rest get an opportunity to meet you and experience your presentation.

Make another list of those who don't like publicity, but are important.
They are important for you want your paintings to be seen when bought.
So when you choose buyers you make sure they are also good sales people.

Ask friends, family, people you know, people you've met, anyone else.
For **THEIR** list of influential people in that community.
They'll also tell you about these people.
Find out why they buy art?

Ask your friends etc. why they've included each person to sort the lists.
If they can't say why – then cross them out.

Combine the two lists.
Ask friends if they know somebody who might know one or two people.
They choose from the combined list.

Ask your friend to call that person (who knows the important person).
Talk to them about anything at all in a short comfortable conversation.
They should mention your name and that you are an extremely talented artist.
Note who will ring whom and relax.

Your word of mouth advertising has begun.

Guarantee buyers with prices that are not high so almost anyone can buy.

If you personally know any collectors, they are VERY important people.

They'll help you get your sell-out exhibition (although they don't know it yet).

4. Who will buy most of your works?

Understand what buyers really do, the selling process is more effective.
How art is sold depends on the buying behaviour typically exhibited by
clients.

Marketing and salesmanship can influence this behaviour.
It's not necessarily the artist's role, and most don't understand it, some do.
BUT the more you understand buying behaviour the more successful you are.

Many artists believe those who pay the highest prices are investors.
Thus they term their major works 'investment art".
On the other hand most people who buy art tend to buy quite a lot.
They're considered art collectors.

Investing implies there'll be a return on the expenditure of money.
When someone invests in shares, bonds, or other financial arrangement.
There's a value for which the investment can be redeemed at any time.
If this value is more than the original outlay the investor gains on redemption.
This return may be money, as in these cases.
The return may also be regular financial payments, such as rent or dividends.
Investment is about making money by capital gains or rent or interest.

Have you seen how valuable some paintings have become?
As a result, they're said to be a great investment.
An art investor should receive similar benefits or they're not investing.
It's difficult to obtain a return on artwork by regular financial payments.
Such as rent or interest (but not impossible).

Most art investors seek a return by rising values or capital gains.
Buy works of little known artists expecting they will be better known in time.
As they becomes better known and more popular, values rise.
The investor has then, at least, made a book profit.
At some point the investor will take their profit by selling the artwork.

It's not certain the artist will be better known, or even their prices rise.
So the investor may buy works by already famous artists.
The expectation is that values will rise even further.

The approaches are like a speculator or a buyer of blue chip stock.
In either case, eventually the investor sells for a profit or to reduce the loss.

Another approach an art investor can use is buy as cheaply as possible.
If one buys (anything) very cheaply there can be an immediate profit.
Investors attend, and buy at art auctions expecting the works will be cheaper.
They buy direct from artists in the expectation they pay less than elsewhere.
This is basically the approach of an art dealer, a buyer and seller of paintings.

The art investor is no different, for investment is about making money.
This applies no matter what the form of investment.
Stocks, shares, land, art, cars, antiques, gold, jewellery are bought.
Then sold to make money.

Are all purchases investments?
If an item is bought with no intention of making money it is not an investment.
Most car buyers are purchasing transport rather than investing in a car.
With stocks and shares, there is no choice but to buy as an investment.

Van Gogh's paintings looked no different when valueless than to-day.
The paintings haven't changed but their monetary value has.
The quality of artwork – whatever that is – is independent of monetary value!

5. How are collectors different?

If an art buyer has no intention of selling, they're not really investing.
If they buy and keep things they love even if it costs money, are collectors.
Collectors get pleasure first and foremost from owning their possessions.
Awareness of rising values can be part, as can indifference to falling values.

Collecting probably started with the caveman.
I imagine bones, stones, and other objects, were collected by some of them.
Just because they liked the look of these things.
Children collect things, at 71/2 years-old, my daughter had a stone collection.
Children's collections survive to adulthood as stamp, coin, or doll collections.

At the other end of the scale is corporate and government collecting.
The latter is usually on a massive scale and costs many millions of dollars.
Public museums and galleries never get smaller only bigger.
There are huge amounts of what is considered most desirable collectibles.
Most of which are then rarely on view, and never sold.

So you can see collecting is a widespread phenomenon.
In fact it's a perfectly natural behaviour to collect objects and items of interest.

Well why do people collect?
It's one of the major ways we make sense of things.

By putting items into categories we start to classify the real world.
Dolls and bears are different.
Stamps and coins share monetary value, but they're different too.
As we sort things into broad groups we notice differences within.
As our knowledge grows, so does the fineness of our classification.
The expert notices things the rest of us miss completely.

Art collecting is, of course, a particular category of collecting.
The objects are things we call art, the most common of these are paintings.
Prints, photographs, sculpture, film and video tapes can be collected as art.

There's no universally accepted definition of what an art object is.
It is plain the field is broad.
There's a branch of philosophy, aesthetics, which considers these questions.
If a person collects what they consider art, then they've an art collection.

The payers of highest prices for artworks are NOT investors.
Investors buy for the lowest price and want to sell at the highest price.
They wait until you reduce your prices, or die, or want discounts.
They want these things so they can make money.

The collector though will pay whatever is needed to get what they want.
The psychology is quite different.

The best art buyers are collectors NOT investors.
Collecting is a compulsive human need.
People collect more of what they collect than otherwise logically justified.
Collecting art is no different.
Collectors can keep you in business.
Be aware of the difference between investors and collectors.
Make it work for you.

What are collectors like?
Investment is **NOT** the motivator.
Collector greed is a powerful driver of art purchases.
They'll want your paintings even more than you want their money.

The collector is not a casual buyer.
They must have.
They also have the money.
But they might have different ethics to you.

It's a business relationship.
So don't expect charity, but it's in the collector's interest to help you.
You don't have to be their friend.
So do business.

Negotiate so not everything goes the collector's way.
Collectors are very hard to put off when they want something.

However investors can still be useful.
They can help kick-start a career by buying when works are cheap.

6. Selling your exhibition idea to the gallery.

After painting works the next major task is sell the idea of an exhibition.
You want an exhibition by yourself at the gallery of your choice.
Fortunately this is not as difficult as you might imagine.
Gallery people are fairly predictable and here's the first thing to keep in mind.
Gallery owners are inundated by artists and artworks.

Something quite different is needed to penetrate their consciousness.
Ignore art industry standard ways (phone for appointment, take portfolio).
They are just art myths for they simply do not work in the majority of cases.
That means forget conventional wisdom.

For this is not how almost any good gallery acquires a new artist!
But you need courage.
If it worth going for, then go for it!

Marketing ideas don't generally improve by delaying implementation.
So don't over-think or over-analyze just get on with it!
Apply pressure to yourself don't delay as that let's worry and doubt creep in.
Set false deadlines if necessary.

Social etiquette has its place.
Selling, whether to the gallery or a prospect, is a people business.
You need to allow people to relax so any consequences are not a concern.
It's a bit like having a fireside chat.

The first step in selling to the gallery is NOT to sell to the gallery.
This still has to happen but not yet!
THEN instead of selling to the gallery sell for the gallery.
Do some of their job for them so it gets very hard for the gallery to say **NO**.
That's why the first step is selling the gallery the idea of an exhibition by you.

7. How do you build credibility?

All this should be done by professionals – not you.
A catalogue of your 20 works in a first class full colour publication.
Your catalogue says they are looking at the work of an important artist.
Your history (just a little bit)
Your philosophy about art (but not too much and in ordinary language)
Something about each painting.

This catalogue is actually a tool to make the following things happen:
Instant sale of the works on the front and back cover.
Progressive sale of the rest.
Provide recognition of you as a professional artist.
Record of first successful exhibition at a leading gallery in the nearest big city.
Publicity for a sell-out show with the buyers as the most important people.
Will help you sell other paintings for years to come.

Don't do it cheap for that will send the wrong message and won't work!
You must invest in yourself if you expect others to.
If you are serious about being an artist you'll find a way.
If you do this exhibition correctly, others pay for everything down the track.

Find someone to write the catalogue.
Study the newspaper you read to get the names of people for your exhibition.
Look at local stories, by-lines, and features to see who writes art stuff.
Do they sign their name to it?

Do you understand what they have written?
If you do, give him/her a call and invite them to lunch.
Show a rough of your catalogue.
Say what you want in a biography, why you're an artist and paint like you do.
Tell them how much this catalogue means to you.

Offer $200 to write and monitor it through to publication.
Ask whether the catalogue is something that could be done by his/her paper?

First choice is a commercial printing department of a newspaper.
The one with the catalogue writer.
This way you get the person and their paper.

The printer might recommend people for photography.
Your first choice is a photographer attached to the same newspaper.

Get the catalogue rolling, so it's properly done.
Inspect progress regularly – looking for accuracy.
Check again and re-do.
If necessary argue (you are a professional remember).
Get the proofs to the journalist, etc.

Now you have a great catalogue under way you can move into top gear.

Chapter Four: Are offers sales?

1. How can you sell more effectively?
2. An offer is setting the stage.
3. Look for the purchase signals.

1. How can you sell more effectively?

You present them for collectors to buy!
People buy most things emotionally.
They rationalize their purchase to explain it to others (even themselves).
Intuition comes before thinking, but only for buyers.
Sellers (you) should know exactly what you are doing.

Start small so eventually the whole idea can appear for your prospect.
There's no need to be smart or trendy or let them know what you know.
It's a good idea to play dumb so use the Colombo (TV detective) strategy.
Then the prospect will reveal all you need to know about how they feel.

Listen for "but" – whatever comes next is important.
Observation is better than relying on listening, watch what actually happens.
Then analyze what you see and hear for clues to the overall process.

You must appeal to the right demographic or your time will be wasted.
But what do you actually do?
Well the idea is to make a presentation to key prospects.

Your presentation should be carefully planned.
Just like any important business presentation for that's exactly what it is.
You offer works for people to buy!

Believe people who praise your work, but remember:
You do **NOT** sell paintings - you offer them.

Paintings don't need to be sold.
They need to be bought.
So you must find the buyer.
But you don't need many.

As you find them and allow them to buy your prices rise.
So you need to sell even less.
But then you are better known.
So people seek you out!

But to find buyers is going to take a lot of time away from the studio.
You will have to do things like:
Checking the market
Developing a list of prospects
Target the best prospects
Prepare a telephone script
Make cold calls
Suggest a time and place for offers
Get referrals

You'll need to find an agent sooner or later.

2. An offer is setting the stage.

Emotional factors are important.
You must engage, entertain and enlighten your prospect.
Set the stage for the perception is the reality.
They need to know you are confident – a winner.
If necessary rent space for the offer.

Rehearse so your offer flows effortlessly.
Go low-tech – don't assume any equipment will work.
Check details
Continually modify to improve your offer.

Avoid complacency and assume nothing.
Know your prospect
Research prospect's business, friends, relatives and anything else relevant.
Then you can relate to the people in the offer.

Leave no stone unturned and have a warm-up act.
Create trust by providing an emotional link before any rational discussion etc.
This must be an entertaining offer.
You must look interested (as must any others in your team).
Allocate roles to team members according to ability (you, agent, spouse).
You can play around with the background or stuff everyone already knows.
Watch for danger signs so if the offer is not working then roll out Plan B

Save the best for last and knock the prospect right out.
Give no handouts – the prospect must experience the major idea.
Have a follow up ready as you might need another way to reach the prospect.

Will the press do a story?
Take advantage of any opportunity.

When planning your offer, make sure you cover just everything.
Run it past other people to check something hasn't been left out.

Details ensure the offer has the correct result – but they must be right.
Sometimes a detail can ignite an unexpected fuse with the prospect.
Often this happens accidentally.

During the offer process allow time for something extra to happen
Everything should contribute to the objective of the offer.
Everything should contribute to your brand identity as well.

3. Look for the purchase signals.

Here are the signs.
Wants to like the work – a lot.
Wants to believe the price paid is a fair one, similar to what others pay.
Wants to actually pay less than that.
Believes you are a professional and one day be better known than now.
Believes you won't quit.
Believes you believe in the work he has because they're all good.
Believes you don't have a better one at home!
Believes the work lasts for generations.
Each generation will thank the original purchaser.
Wants others to like it – a lot.
Knows about supply and demand.
You are not prolific, you'll die in due course and then big $$$ down the track.

Buyers have money to buy paintings.
Understand that good paintings have monetary value.
Like to look at paintings and get something from the experience.
Like to own things they like to look at (collector).

So arrange for the buyer to spend time with the painting (not paintings).
All collectors are at least one painting away from completing their collection.
Like to display things they own and have a place to do so.
Want to be admired and understood for what they own and collect over years.
Their collection is their art as it communicates about them.

Most buyers are middle-aged to elderly.
Have well-established careers in which they are active or comfortably retired.
Had parents who valued and/or collected paintings etc.
Their children often inherit collections but also the drive as well.
Are probably well educated.
Their collection could be an aspect of their on-going education.
Read books and have them around and support other arts.
Don't waste your time on anyone else – they want to monopolize your time.

People will not buy if they:
Like everything you show them.
Tell you they just love art.
Have a wife or husband who does all the art buying.
Are other artists.
Are starving, poor, and generally have no money.
Don't like what you do, your agent, you, or your price.
Are members of school parent groups.
Are politicians.
Are ex-buyers who are experiencing changed circumstances?

But - people do change!

Try these tests?
Do they want to look at the painting or hear you talk?
When they are looking do they really see the work or talk?
They can't do both?
When looking, are they reminded of a relative who paints?
If so then they're not interested in yours.
How long does the prospect spend with each work?
The more time the better (speed readers don't buy)!
Ask the prospect to take it closer to the natural light.
Tell the prospect to lean the work against the wall and step back for a look.
How was it placed down?

The prospect should treat the work as if it is a car bomb.

Selling more:
Engage the prospect in conversation and ask about their interests.
Take them to a special viewing room.
Show the chosen work on a felt draped easel, with key spot lighting.
Have coffee and a comfortable viewing chair, etc.
There are more sales than hanging in a gallery that doesn't know what to do.

Even the successful gallery has a problem.
A client's attention is divided by the number of artists represented.
Some will barely receive wall space.
A gallery will spend most of their time selling the works they know will sell.
Your art is different so it will take time for their clients to get used to it.

Selling even more:
Don't open your own gallery.
You won't be able to afford the space for buyers to walk through.
When you can you won't want to!
Your gallery is a second floor office with a phone and a computer.
The dealer is on the phone looking for clients.
You or your agent can do that from home.

But you do know art is a business!
You paint the works and sell them.
You own the inventory and the copyright.
You don't have to sell many.
They're easy to transport.
Just get reasonable value for cash.

Chapter Five: Move into top gear
1. Find the movers and shakers.
2. It is time to sell to the gallery!
3. Contact the three movers and shakers again.
4. Talk to the journalist again.

1. Find the movers and shakers.

For a while now you have been collecting people's names.
So you should know who the real movers and shakers of culture are.
In the city where your exhibition will be held.

Well how do you identify these people?
They're at fund-raising events for charities with something to do with the arts.
They preside over balls and organize auctions.
They organize membership drives for museums, public galleries, etc.
They get theatre groups to stage events for the poor, people with aids, etc.

They're all women and each commands a loyal group of volunteers.
Be nice to these people or you will blow the whole exhibition project.
If you are very nice they can help you – a lot.

Time for tea and biscuits with movers and shakers of exhibition city!

Phone your first mover and shaker.
Tell her you've read of all her good works and know of her interest in the arts
And how important she is to the community.
Tell her you've an art project to benefit the community and you'd like advice.

It's a visual offer in the fine arts so it's hard to convey over the phone.
You want to take her to lunch or tea so you can show it to her.
Failing that you'll meet her anywhere at her convenience.
If you do well you'll have lunch but do whatever is needed to get to meet her.

Do the same with two more mover and shakers.

Now you will have to definitely select that gallery!
Make sure it's the best one.
The work they show is not unlike yours.
It's not going out of business.

Have lunch/tea with each mover and shaker.
Choose a quiet restaurant.
Show her the catalogue as well as the two cover originals (front & back).
Allow her to be enthusiastic.
Tell her about your art project (see below).
Give her a catalogue.
Sign and date underneath nice words you've composed about meeting her.

The project is a one-man exhibition in the gallery you have selected.
When you discuss it with a gallery owner you'd like to use her as reference.
THAT'S IT!

No you don't want to sell her one of your paintings.
You only have 20 and they're all reserved for the exhibition.
The mover and shaker will be relieved.

If she likes the works (even a bit) she'll say yes.
She'll even agree to write a few lines of praise of your work and sign it.
You brought some stationery and a pen.

When you get to mover and shaker three you'll be the talk of the town.

2. Now it is time to sell to the gallery!

What do you want from the gallery?
Well you are no longer just trying to be accepted by your gallery.
You want a one-man exhibition.
You want it soon.
You want it done your way.

Call for an appointment.
It's courtesy.
It's professional.

You'll need to overcome gallery bias.
Artists don't know about business (most don't).
Artists will not conform to established business practices.

But what if they don't want to see you?
They're too busy.
They're not interested in new artists right now, whatever.

Tell him you're busy too.
You're in the same business let's see if we can find five minutes together?
You want to discuss what is important to both of us – making money!

What if they want you to send samples of your work?
Send **ONE**.
This should be **TYPICAL** of most of your works.
But this is unlikely if the ladies and artists have done their job.

When you get an appointment:
Arrive on time – that's essential.
Make a professional, business-like presentation.
Be organized logically and thoughtfully (see elsewhere).

Dress in keeping with the making money nature of the business.
Show the catalogue and the colour slides used for it.
Take about six original stretched paintings.
They are numbered and titled on the back.
Also the endorsements by the three mover and shakers.

Walk the gallery owner through the colour catalogue.
This might be better than the gallery owner has produced for his artists.

He'll know the three women who endorsed you exhibiting there.
They'll be clients or he wished they were.
He'll know about their supporters and how many will come to your exhibition
A second-rate gallery will not know these things.

He'll note how you acknowledged the importance of the gallery.
That's when he said he couldn't schedule an exhibition for at least a year.
Normally there's a 2 or 3 year wait.
He'll take in how you said you only needed a Saturday and Sunday.
Or four working days in the art season.

You know like he does schedules change for a good enough reason.
Point out that you are ready now.
You only need time to frame the works and catalogues with invites mailed.

You'll make it clear you understand how hard it is to sell a new artist.
That's why you've spent so much time, effort and money on the catalogue.
That's also why those 20 or so works retail at an average of only $500 each.

Commit to building a market in his gallery and know sacrifices involved.
You'll tell him you'll do the framing and have them ready for hanging.
They're already catalogued by price and size.
You'll accept his terms of a 60/40 split or whatever he suggests.
A new artist you may be offered 50/50 so fight it – fight it but accept it.
You'll agree to give him the gallery commission whenever sales take place.

You'll add your mailing list to his.
Some help will come from the three mover and shakers.
Expect him to pay for invitation mailing, advertising and the opening.
You may have to give some ground here as well.

You have invested in this project you want to make sure it's successful.
You'll pursue sales yourself in the community.

Do NOT promise but you'll want to sell the lot before the opening.
He's seen the offer (which you practiced) so he knows you might do that.
There's always a week between scheduled shows too.
So it doesn't have to alter his timetable if he doesn't want to.
He can pay for a small ad, and not much for invitations.

The big expense is the mailing but it's a promotion for the gallery.
He could earn money from other sales.
He will also get in good with the movers and shakers and their supporters.

BUT what if in spite of all your efforts you get nowhere?
Ask for a reference to a gallery more likely to be interested in what you do.
Ask them to ring that gallery to make an appointment for you.

BUT you'll get your exhibition!

3. Contact the three movers and shakers again.

Meet them one by one.
Personally deliver the invitation if it's ready – otherwise a verbal invitation.
Bring some flowers for each M&S.

The three women are now members of your team.
Bring works most interest shown in (2/3) when they looked at the catalogue.
Just in case they'd like to see the actual paintings.
Generously offer a chance to buy, but only if hung in exhibition with red spot.

There's a discreet sign (not too much) "For Mr & Mrs (name) collection"
They'll all know if they buy now – they buy cheap!
That's because your prices do not yet reflect your growing status.

What if they want a painting from the front or back of the catalogue?
Sell for a premium ($100 or $200) above the average for similar sized works.
M&S1, M&S2 or M&S3 refer you to friends they don't reject the invitation.

In return for their help you will agree to speak at each of their women's clubs.
Your talk will be based on your exhibition.
You'll have invitations available and a copy of the catalogue at nominal cost.

Suggest to whichever M&S that in her introduction she might mention.
Stay behind to discuss painting purchases with anyone who is interested.
When you talk thank Mrs. M&S and mention she is one of your collectors.

By your exhibition, everyone will have heard of you.

4. Talk to the journalist again.

Show him/her a finished catalogue and sign a copy.
Tell him/her about sales to M&S 1, 2 and 3 and show their endorsements.

Suggest as the exhibition approaches the newspaper runs a story.
Also the opening reception is rapidly becoming a "social event."
If he/she won't, or can't, cover this, ask to be introduced to someone who will.

You'd like a picture of yourself and someone famous (now or later).
Quotes not from you but the gallery owner (if reporter asks?).
Don't write about the art at all (leave that for people to judge).
The trendy set are looking for drawing power – so let's organize that.

Chapter Six: Sell the exhibition

1. Now use your contact lists (remember them).
2. Make the offer.
3. Some potential comments and your responses.
4. Go flat out selling while there are any left to sell.

1. Now use your contact lists (remember them).

It's time to talk to prospects.
You have a big carrot to offer potential buyers (prospects).
A scheduled exhibition in a leading gallery in the nearest big city!

Use your friends to get past gatekeepers to very important people (VIP).
Check with friends to make sure they called the VIP contact as promised.
Did they mention your name and that you are a talented artist?

Now phone the VIP's.
You will have to start with the VIP's gatekeeper (secretary, receptionist).
When you ask to talk to the VIP mention your friend and a mutual friend.

If asked, explain that you don't know the VIP but your good friend does.
Add that your good friend recently talked to the VIP about you as an artist.
Both the VIP and your friend will verify this if necessary.

Once you talk to the VIP the aim is an appointment to meet at his office.
You must sound rational and business–like on the phone.
Say you don't want to waste his time so just mention these points:

He probably doesn't often receive calls about art.
He might like it or feel he should.
He is a VIP because he listens to others and learns from them.
You can teach him a little in a non-threatening environment (his).
He's heard of Mrs. M&S 1, 2, and 3 as well as the gallery.
He may owe his wife or someone else a gift and likes to shop at his office.

He may know how his company can benefit.

If they purchase the entire collection or part of it.

If he gets interested there'll be more time.

He's smart so he'll have ideas you haven't even thought of.

Your suggestions get him thinking.

You'll get to see him but you'll get just 5 minutes to show some paintings.

AND make him understand what a good and valuable artist you are.

BUT if he gets interested there'll be more time.

Arrive on time and in suitable clothes and hairstyle.

Conduct all offers, wherever held, as if each will be the last meeting.

Say nice things to secretary, you may come again but not anything important!

Carry everything for your offer into the office with you.

You may need several trips from your car to the secretary.

But move into the office with the lot.

This shows you have gone to some trouble.

Be organized and have things ready to show (you did practice didn't you?).

Use portfolios, attaché cases or whatever is needed, but not shopping bags.

2. Make the offer.

Start as soon as you're invited into the office and exchanged greetings.
Be ready to answer questions about why you have created what you present.
Do **NOT** give long answers, ask return questions, find out about the prospect.

Don't waste time trying to be the prospect's friend.
You want a client and there is a significant difference.

Don't wait until the conversation turns to 'Well what have you brought?'
Use "I" very sparingly during the offer.

Let the prospect set the pace.
Watch carefully and listen as well.
If he doesn't like something put it away and don't refer to it again.
Tell the prospect the paintings are for sale and also the price.
Art is a visual experience, so guide him.
Very briefly tell him what you have, and show the paintings one at a time.
As he looks – under the best light you can organize

SHUT UP and STAND BACK.
Don't talk about anything at all.
Let him begin a love affair.
Leave him alone.
Don't rush another painting.

BUT WATCH!
When you sense restlessness, tell him something about the painting.
Where it was painted, why it's how it is, etc.

BUT not too much!
The longer he looks the better he will remember it.
Then take it away and produce another one.
Handle the paintings in a way that conveys value and reverence.
Consider investing in white gloves!

Make sure any gallery or dealer handles them the same way.

You must talk money to make money.
There will be no sale unless you talk money – it's that simple!
Start by seeking group sales (lot, three, etc.) but if necessary settle for one.
If investment potential has been demonstrated multiple sales are possible.

Selling at low prices is a getting started strategy NOT an on-going one.
Be prepared to negotiate.
Say "Those are the prices for individual works.
Buy the collection, or a group of four (or more), then I'll consider price again.
It is worth something not to return for a second try so consider reductions.

Don't give any second figure.
You've made your offer – it's up to him to counter.

You are a presenter and guide so ask questions.
Let him tell you what he likes about the painting.

Narrow the choices if only one is being bought.
Expand the choices if more than one is being purchased.
Your prospect will be direct, so you should be too – this is business!

You believe in your art and you are doing the prospect a favour.
It should be clear your prices won't hold their present level.
Believe this and convey it to the prospect.
When he buys he'll thank you for helping him.

Work out the number of paintings you'll sell for the art budget.
Don't worry about being "pushy" for no-one will buy if they don't want to.
Until the prospect says "No" then assume they're saying "Maybe".
Continue to ask questions and maintain contact.
Ask if he's decided yet?

The opposite is doing nothing in which case nothing will happen.
You will have access to exclusive boardrooms and plush homes.
Don't be overwhelmed.

3. Some potential comments and your responses.

I just don't know anything about art.
You like the prospect's frankness.
Briefly, tell him what you are doing and what art is.
Ask if he feels anything from any painting?
Which does he feel strongest about?

I need time to think it over.
Ask why and for how long.

I like it but I have cash-flow problems over the next few months.
Judge credit worthiness.
Do you want to sell for a substantial down-payment and rest in three months?
Explain he'll have to sign a sales contract which you show.
The contract is painting and money **BOTH** lost if 3 month payment missed.
He'll understand this as it's what he'd do too.

Will the colour or style conforms to the room where I'd like to hang it?
Say **YES** but not just because you want to sell the painting.
It's true as a painting has its own space and commands its own attention.

4. Go flat out selling while there are any left to sell.

When you get money immediately divide it as per the gallery contract.
Pay the gallery owner his share.
The gallery owner will not believe it!
He'll also feel guilty.
He'll increase the size of his ad and do a few things that he wasn't going to.

He'll feel some pressure to make sales.
This might be preserve status as he doesn't want a new artist to out-sell him!
Put your share of the money towards framing the works.
Keep all receipts and relevant paperwork.

Your deadline is the start of the opening – that's the end of sales!
At openings people talk about buying paintings – but don't usually buy.
If you're lucky there might be one or two sales.
The gallery owner or staff may sell – but don't count on it!

But you need a gallery opening for that's how people think art is sold.
This is an illusion – but it works for you and other smart art people.
People like to go to openings before they go out to dinner or take in a show.
A countdown to the opening determines time for buying in advance (preview).

Continue making offers
Talk to everyone you know
Get a catalogue to anyone who is interested.

Check regularly with the gallery owner.
Co-ordinate efforts with the gallery owner.
Pay the gallery owner as the money is received.
Check the gallery owner promoted your exhibition on all available radio spots.
Later check on the papers.

Make sure the gallery owner followed through with calls to HIS list.
Find out what he hasn't done and offer to do it but this could be a lot!

Ask people have they received their catalogues and invitations.
Say you are looking forward to meeting them at the opening.
Tell them there are still some paintings not bought yet.
You don't want them at the opening expecting the selection you offer now.
You will show any from the catalogue provided they aren't been sold already.
You'll come to their home, or meet them somewhere for an hour or so.

Go to your place of worship.
Talk to the priest, rabbi, minister, whatever, and tell him what you are doing.
Talk in detail about your work.
Talk him through the catalogue and invite him to the opening.
Ask if he knows any parishioners who'd like a catalogue and leave him some.
OK you are almost there now.

Ask people have they received their catalogues and invitations.
Say you are looking forward to meeting them at the opening.
Tell them there are still some paintings not bought yet.
You don't want them at the opening expecting the selection you offer now.
You will show any from the catalogue provided they aren't been sold already.
You'll come to their home, or meet them somewhere for an hour or so.

Go to your place of worship.
Talk to the priest, rabbi, minister, whatever, and tell him what you are doing.
Talk in detail about your work.
Talk him through the catalogue and invite him to the opening.
Ask if he knows any parishioners who'd like a catalogue and leave him some.
OK you are almost there now.

Chapter Seven: Wrapping up.

1. Do you know how to behave at your exhibition opening?

How will you go at the opening?
Arrive sober, and don't drink or eat at the opening, as neither helps sales.
You are the guest of honour.

You come early and leave late.
You thank everyone for coming.
You graciously acknowledge all compliments.
You do this by smiling and saying "Thank you" or "Glad you like it".
Or even "I'd enjoy seeing your daughter's first painting" etc.

Dress for the occasion, stay in a corner with none of your paintings.
You want people to see your work,avoid problems, stay in neutral corner.

You'll be introduced to lots of people, so be polite.
Buyers like to meet you but after they've bought not before.

Otherwise they're in a compromised situation.
They won't talk freely about the work.
Or why they like it, nor state an opinion.
So play that ace after they've bought if possible (so they buy again).

If approached (loudly) by someone who wants a work already sold.
Don't refer her to a painting that hasn't been sold.

Ask her to point out the painting.
Then ask her to point out the painting in the catalogue.
Look puzzled, then concerned and finally relieved.

Tell her you think there's a mistake which she has helped discover.
Tell her the painting is available.
All she needs to do is take her money to the gallery owner.
Point him out and you won't see her again!

2. Now what!

If setting up the sell-out worked and there weren't many discounts
You may have only broke-even but for a start-up venture that's excellent.

Your approximate costs:

Colour separations and catalogue printing	$	3500
Framing	$	1000
Photographs	$	200
Lunch/tea	$	100
Fine for unauthorised fire	$	50
Flowers	$	150
Miscellaneous	$	200
Total:	$	5200

Your approximate income:

Sales 20 works @ $500 each average price	$	10,000
Less gallery commission 40%	$	4,000
Total	$	6,000
Your profit:	$	800

BUT ...
You have a great catalogue which can help you sell into the future.
A continuing market, with the gallery anticipating the next sell-out.
Photos and publicity for future use.
An education you won't get any other way.
Credibility as an artist (with only 20 paintings).
You've had a successful one-man exhibition at a leading gallery.
Last exhibition was a sell-out.
And that's just the start!
It was never going to be easy.

You can leverage this start.
You are on your way.
How far do you want to go?

3. Future exhibitions.

There are three phases for a sell-out exhibition at any gallery.
Painting works (about 20) with careful consideration to the size.
Selling the exhibition to the gallery (starts when most works are ready).
Sell the exhibition for the gallery.
They won't do it for unknown artists so you must.

You know how long the first phase will take.
The other two phases could easily take three months.
They will involve quite a deal of non-painting time from you (or your agent).

At the end of a first sell-out exhibition at that gallery you will have:
No works
No money
No debt

Then get started on sell-out exhibition no 2 at that or another gallery.
Painting the works (about 20 again).

This will be easier because of the first sell-out exhibition.
The gallery will be keen to cash in on your slightly higher prices.

At the end of your second sell out exhibition at any gallery you have:
No works
Some money (slightly higher prices and reduced costs)
No debt

Now you get started on sell-out exhibition no 3.
Painting the works (about 20 with some a little larger).
Selling the exhibition to the gallery only if it's a new gallery.

This will be even easier because of your track record.
Your agent can do this even while you are painting the works.
It might be one of the first two galleries, who'll already have keen buyers.
Selling the exhibition by the gallery.
Your agent tells new galleries how to do it.
Then they cash in on your success.

At the end of a third sell out exhibition at a prestige gallery you have:
No works
Even more money (slightly higher prices again).
Plus some larger works at even higher prices, with minimal costs.
No debt

This process repeats, only limited by the number of works you paint.
So all you have to do is paint and keep track of your agent.
You will need an agent by then so you can paint.
The prices will keep moving up.
You reach a stage where you are embarrassed by the dollars they bring in.

Three elements in an exhibition can be varied to cater for demand.
The size of works, the price of the works and the number of each size.
Different combinations can cater for increased or decreased demand.
But still be able to continue to exhibit successfully in the future.

If demand for your works is high (lots of interest).
Then increase prices, but only just a bit so you don't kill the golden goose.
Also increase the size of works available.
Keep the number of works available the same.

If demand for your works is lower (less interest).
Then decrease the number of works available.

Also decrease the size of works available.
Keep the prices the same so you don't kill the golden goose.

4. Next time think about a preview period.

The selling phase is more usually called a Preview Period.
Sales activity is focused on individuals who might buy.
During this time early buying is encouraged.

Do this by early notification of your exhibition to keen buyers.
AND special preview prices.
Mailings reinforce this phase.
Which ends when the exhibition opens to the public.

The next sales phase is more often called the Exhibition Period.
An exhibition opening is a transition from a sales to a public display mode.
The exhibition phase is when future sales prospects can be identified.
General publicity during the exhibition is more likely to attract such people.
How work is displayed may reflect a difference of the phases (also price).

Could you use incentive pricing?
Incentive pricing can be implemented during the selling or preview phase.
The main focus of marketing exhibitions is to generate multiple sales.
Incentive pricing rewards early buyers.
The best (lowest) price is for preview period buyers, buy later pay most.

Pricing is thus used as a tactic to encourage earlier decision making.
It encourages people to buy when you want them to rather than take time.
An objective is sell as many works as possible before the formal opening.
That means the lot.

The initial price (lowest) must be considered carefully.
This is your ordinary selling price, but in this situation it could be less.
The later exhibition price must be higher.

Just how much higher depends on you and your gallery.
It may be a token amount.
Or it may vary according to the price of the works.
At my gallery we used to have a 10% difference between the two prices.
You and your gallery must sell before your opening.
Otherwise there's no point in incentive pricing.
It's part of the pre-selling strategy.
Your later prices could be 10% higher.
Even in this first exhibition!

In addition to selling how can you help?
Help a gallery implement incentive pricing.
They shouldn't have any price on the back of works.
If you wrote the higher price perhaps it would not matter much.
Then all prices are 10% (or whatever) above what you really want.
A client takes a painting home and discovers a higher price, a bargain.

Eventually your price could vary between different galleries?
This doesn't matter!
You are educating people to buy at your **NEXT** exhibition.
This sort of educational process is better with works that didn't sell (if any).
Than with a whole bunch of new works in your next exhibition.
If all works are sold at the pre-opening incentive price.
Print a new catalogue.
This has higher prices for use at the opening and the rest of the exhibition.

The point is to provide an incentive for people to buy early.
Also to build price rise expectations ahead of future exhibitions.

5. Don't forget the red spots!

Usually at an exhibition opening red spots are placed on sold works.
This tells people which ones are sold and which are not.
The idea is people will select from the unsold paintings.
But does this actually happen?
To some extent it does, or there would be no further sales.
But notice how sales diminish from this point too.
People say they'd have bought a work but it was already sold!
It's a pretty common statement isn't it?
These people certainly haven't made their selection from unsold works.
They've made it from the whole exhibition.

Well, what if people could only see the unsold works?
When the works are sold, remove from the exhibition, take them down.
Then people couldn't fall in love with ones that aren't available.
They'd judge the unsold works on their merits.
They'd have to guess about what the sold ones may have been like.

This is what the used car dealer does.
He drives the just sold car away from the car lot.
He knows, any other people who fall in love with this car, can't have it.
He doesn't want that to happen.
A new car dealer leaves them on the showroom floor, as he can get more.

Red spots in place of the actual paintings still signify sold works.
It's possible you have an exhibition with only a few unsold works, or none!
It'd look terrible.
But be a great promotion for the exhibition and future ones by you too.
People remember and talk about this kind of thing.

After a sale.

Works are taken by buyers or put in storage if not paid for.

Then you're likely to get paid quicker too.

Clients who collect their purchase earlier are clients who also paid faster.

Maybe at an opening re-hang sold works not taken by new owners.

Then this is a special event.

In this case following the opening the sold works are taken down again.

But there's little point having people fall in love with works they can't have.

6. But first what happens to your past?

You are now in a new career, as a well-known and successful artist.
What will those works that belong to your old career do now?
You must distance yourself from those works.
Otherwise they'll undermine your new status.

The best way is to do this publicly and dramatically.
Find all your old paintings – the lot.
You no longer need them as insurance in case something goes wrong.
Now you have momentum with your work and these are not part of it.

But first sort out your paintings sketches and prints.
Keep these ones:
Those that represent your new way.
Those that you intend to keep and not sell (superannuation or pension).
Very good frames in sizes you can re-use.
Sketches relevant to new works, some prints, give away in promotions.

Look carefully at those old works.
Are there any as good as the latest works?
If you are really sure about that then put them aside.
Don't forget the works you removed from their frames.

All the rest get burnt.
Your new paintings now are the equivalent of actual cash.
So the old ones can't be given away.
To maintain the cash value of your works ALL must be your best.
But be quite objective and single-minded about this.
Burn most prints to improve dramatically the edition as "sold out".
In future do not print anything like that number.

Your future depends on not letting a single work out of your sight.
That's if it is not to your latest standard.

Have a party where you live.
Invite your neighbours as well as the press.
Choose a fine week-end morning when there are plenty of people about.

Take the lesser works out into your front yard, or street if necessary.
BURN them along with warped and damaged stretchers and frames.
If a spectator wants one free – refuse.

Hold up each painting dramatically for all then throw it on the fire.
Pretend you are a priest of an obscure faith.
Each sacrifice is accompanied by a ritual.
Burn each work and frame one at a time.
That takes longer and is more spectacular.
Dress suitably but not weird as you are a responsible and sensible artist.

If people want your fire permit – reply saying what you are doing.
You are celebrating your turning point as an artist by burning your past.
Invite those people to your opening reception.
Set up a table so you can sign the catalogues.

Police come due to the fire, tell them what you're doing.
Tell them about the upcoming exhibition and Invite them too.
Give them a catalogue.

When the fire burns out, sweep up the ashes.
Put them in a container you have brought.
Gather your table and the catalogues and move to your house.

Without a glance backward wave to those still gathered at the scene.

Years ago a well-known Australian artist did this kind of thing.
Although I remember the event my recollections of the details are sketchy.
Not like they would be now.

The important thing is, I've never forgotten this either.
It's a dramatic statement in a field like ours.
Works assume magical properties due to the creative process.
Use this common myth to your advantage as you start a new career.

7. Why do people come to your exhibitions?

Do you want to earn a living from your art?
Then they come to buy one of your works (at least).
OK how do you know that's why they are there?
Mostly you don't for usually you just hope enough of them are there.

Well is there something you can do to fix this problem?
Normally you send out invitations to lots of people who might buy.
But you spend money on lots of people who will not buy too.
Same thing goes for any advertising.
How can you improve on this?

To start with make sure you invite people who are most likely to buy.
That is those who have bought before.
It's also those who have bought most recently – not ten years ago.
The very best are those who paid most.

OK but who else can you invite?
Well it all depends on what you are inviting them to.
If it is the exhibition then anyone might do.

But what if it is for an opportunity to preview the exhibition?
Now that would be different wouldn't it?
Particularly if there was an opportunity to actually buy works then!
Obviously those previous buyers can be invited and they should be.
It is a reward for their past support.

What about everyone else?
They need some sorting out don't they?
Start the sorting by asking people to register for the coming exhibition.

Then at least you know people who register are interested.
Invite them to an early viewing opportunity available to people registered.

After people have registered provide them with a printed catalogue.
This has exhibition prices and images.

Also let them know they will receive a registered buyer's discount.
This is 10% less than the catalogued price.
But they do have to buy **BEFORE** the exhibition opens.

Once the exhibition opens invite registration for the NEXT exhibition.
You could even outline the benefits of registration.
Continue this process while the exhibition is open to the public.

Then you should have registered buyers for your next exhibition.
Before your present exhibition has closed!
Do you think that would improve your sales then?
Would it also improve your chances of having another exhibition as well?

What if those future exhibitions are also successful?
Would you keep seeking interested buyer registration?

WHERE NEXT:

BUT being a professional artist is NOW harder than it ever was. These books are on earning money from a professional art career.

Gallery Co-Operation
http://www.amazon.com/dp/B087637FFW

Selling Strategies
http://www.amazon.com/dp/B0882JH3WN

Copyright
http://www.amazon.com/dp/B0892HWYTV

Art Hiring
http://www.amazon.com/dp/B0884JWR2S

Agents
http://www.amazon.com/dp/B08847Y9KS

Your Website
http://www.amazon.com/dp/B08846SWQP

Courses and Workshops
http://www.amazon.com/dp/B0884B51JB

Selling Prints
http://www.amazon.com/dp/B08846SWQW

Retirement
http://www.amazon.com/dp/B0884D9TBP

Art School
http://www.amazon.com/dp/B08849FV59

TAKE THE PLUNGE and Consider a Gallery.
http://www.amazon.com/dp/B0874JF964
Hardback
http://www.amazon.com/dp/B09GQRB34T

NOT NOW:

Perhaps one of these books could interest you then?

Write a book about your own memories.
YOU could publish it then – like I did!
http://www.amazon.com/dp/B087DWKPTP

A simple way to start developing creativity.
If you are a parent, teacher or someone who meets a group regularly?
http://www.amazon.com/dp/B088T1KFQZ

This is the way most people start to become an artist!
http://www.amazon.com/dp/B088Y1DPL6

Some more of my memories.
http://www.amazon.com/dp/B088Y4RPL9

SEND TO:

Know anyone interested in chocolate recipes?
Send them this link then.
http://www.amazon.com/dp/B0882HK9Q9

Know anyone interested in THIS book?
They can set up a sell-out!
http://www.amazon.com/dp/B0882MFPGX

www.ingramcontent.com/pod-product-compliance
Lightning Source LLC
Chambersburg PA
CBHW020559220526
45463CB00006B/2377